Change your life - Be happy and In Love in 30 Days
guaranteed

ALL Woman Alone

USE OUR Magic Grand Slam Plan

"GET YOUR MAN!"

Joan McCormack, AUTHOR
Thomas McCormaek Publisher

"GET YOUR MAN!!"

USE THE "MAGIC GRAND SLAM PLAN"
Start Now – You will be "happy and in love."

Within 30 Days- GUARANTEED!!
Authored by Thomas and Joan McCormack

INTRODUCTION

This forward is being written to invite the readers of this fine masterpiece to prepare for the most direct, outright finished details of how to change your life now and your whole future development by investing first the time to read, then the time to plan your exciting future with the making the commitment to fulfill what may in the past have been a faraway dream.

The author is specific in detail, and her plans should be followed tightly. When that happens, I can assure you of the success ahead.

I am writing this as a final seal of approval because I'm the guy that this author landed over 25 years ago, and I played my part correctly because here I am. I am no actor. I was, at the time, an open-minded traveling salesman who stopped overnight for a meal and a night's sleep. And Bam! There she was, and I was hooked!

The author is my best friend and the only love-of-my-life I've ever had, and we've not been apart since we met.

Best wishes in your reading and executing of the plans for the rest of your life.

Sincerely, Tom McCormack

Thomas & JoAn McCormack, Authors of nine other books on Kindle.

"Dear Reader,

Please fill out the information requested below and send it to us at 16775 Joshua Tree Lane, Hudson, FL 34667 as soon as possible.

We have a Special Gift for you:

I will personally CALL you within the first week and will send you your <u>Personal Bio</u>. You can use it as is, add to it, change as you wish, but USE it to join one of the Dating Sites and choose a "man' as you wish to meet; or for the excited man to find you, who wants to meet you soon,....... if not sooner!"

Name _____

Address _____

Email Address _____

**Local Phone Number _____

Do you like to:

Read..... Yes/No....

Sew..... Yes/No....

Travel.... Yes/No....

Eat Out.... Yes/No....

Go To Movies..... Yes/No....

Swim..... Yes/No

Sports….. Yes/No…. What? _____

Have Hobbies….. Yes/No…. What? _____

Are you "Electric"…. Yes/No….

Well-traveled…. Yes/No….

Thank you, I look forward to talking to you soon! JoAn

Colin and Judy Howse – Met on-line, Married in April, 2021.

Ricky Dziezic and Kaitie Livingood met on-line at "Facebook Daters"! They felt that they were a good match and made a date. Ricky told himself: "Go Big" so he made a reservation at a very nice Japanese restaurant. They have been going out every weekend to sports events and local museums. Katie told me they have been dating a year and are very happy. Their careers are going fine and they are very happy together and their personal lives are just great!

Just think, Dear Reader, The "Grand Slam Offer" in this book is to guarantee you will be happy and "in love," maybe sooner if you are ready to get up and Go.......... Dress up .... Join .... And Go OUT, you will land your man in just 30 days. In just 30 days, that's right!

30 Days

4 Weeks

One Month!

You are going on an intensive program, a full-blown assault! Put yourself on a fast track while staying close to home. Your dream is coming true.

You deserve the best in your "golden years" or in any year! Just 30 days to discover your newest "male friend." Guaranteed!

WE'RE OFF!

WEEK #1 – Getting "beautiful" in mind and body, what fun!

WE'RE OFF! WEEK #1 – Getting "Beautiful" in mind and body, what fun! I HAD JUST STARTED READING MY NEWEST BOOK, TITLED "$100M" In Your First Year! The first words caught my eye and, as I was reading, I saw the words, "Hungry Audience," my mind said: NO, not a hungry audience, the book says a really hungry audience, so I came up with "A STARVING AUDIENCE"! The book was pointing the way. Tom and I started thinking hard about this "Starving Audience." Well, without

LONELY WOMEN

SINGLE WOMEN

WIDOWED WOMEN

UNHAPPILY MARRIED WOMEN

LONELY

LONELY WOMEN - OUR READER..... LONELY FOR ALL THE

THINGS THAT MAKE A HAPPIER LIFE!"

We BECAME EXCITED – We HAD FOUND THE PERFECT AUDIENCE, AND, NOW WHAT? Get Published and start selling – getting it to the audience!

WOW!!! That will be some business! And, just think, you are going to be a part of it. After you get this book, the very first thing you need to do right now

(DO IT NOW) Is to go out to our E-mail and sign up for our club. This way, you will get a personal invite to celebrate at our Book Sellers Celebration Party u, um – think of all the single people who will be there – looking for their man!

(islanders2j@gmail.com)

At this time, I don't have a clue. What? What? Who knows? What? Do you? Yes – You, Our Reader!

Do you know? It is just selling our books, or do we need to do more? What would it be? Do you have an idea? YES?

If so, please, please, call us at 1(321) 536-6555 and tell us –

The only thing we are doing is writing our book for our audience, excuse us................ OUR "STARVING AUDIENCE":

Yes, we have it – YOU – THE READER are our "STARVING AUDIENCE" – Yes, "YOU"!

We are almost afraid to write it down; someone will steal it and become rich!

THIS is our "STARVING AUDIENCE":

"Women who are LONELY................................be they:

>   Single

>   Widowed or

>   Unhappily married women.

>   Lonely women who need a

>   Friend

>   Companion

>   MAN!"

This book is intended to be informational. You will read through, coming back again and again. Each time you will gain new knowledge. To work, you need "tools." This book is full of all the "tolls" needed to "Get Your Man!"

Yes, women who need, or just want (for the fun of it!), a man (person) to help do things around the house (like mow the lawn, paint, fix things, etc.) you know the type – Handyman!

Friend

Companion

Man

To go with you on a:

Short trip

Long trip

Overseas trip

Train trip

Boat trip

Movies

Fine dining

Lunches

Even going to the theatre!

So many things to do AND no one to do them with – well …

LET US HELP YOU WITH OUR MAGIC "GRAND SLAM OFER".

Let us help you find your:

Soulmate

Friend

Companion

Man…….. In just 30 days – Yes, that's right – JUST 30 DAYS!

Guaranteed (Just do the things outlined in this book. That's all, JUST FOLLOW the book, and your life will be CHANGED) – IN JUST 30 DAYS

<u>GUARANTEED!</u>

When you believe your Social Status will be increased among your peers, our "Starving Audience" will be drooling! Look at the benefits in terms of Status aimed from the viewpoint of other.

That's the SECRET! How others will perceive the reader's (your) Achievements.

We will connect the DOTS for you.

EXAMPLE: if you buy this golf club (Man), your drive (chances) will increase by 40 yards. Your friends' jaws will drop when they see your ball (SOAR 40 yards beyond theirs) you on the arm of that great looking man!!

This is the perceived <u>Likelihood of Achievement (GOAL – INCREASE).</u> People want CERTAINTY! Perceived likelihood of getting what you want!

Believing our OFFER will actually WORK for YOU will increase your convictions that OUR offer is very, very valuable!

<u>Increase Value!</u> To increase value, we must communicate and believe the likelihood of your achieving success through our messaging. Proof that what we choose to include or exclude in our offer and our guarantees will increase the intensity of your life a million times. Your friend and acquaintances' jaws will drop when they see you "stepping out" on the arm of that well-dressed, successful man....again and again! AND, then, marriage! Well, um, m, m

Yes! YES!

TIME DELAY - FIRST DATE

We want you to have a "big" emotional win" early as possible (close as possible to your reading this book). It takes a while to achieve a "first date." That's what you are reading - now there is a need to create your "emotional win" FAST! One way to get your life in "high gear" is to get you to go out on your FIRST DATE IN THE FIRST 7 days!

TRUST US!

By framing the benefits in terms of Status gained from the viewpoint of others, will make you believe you will increase your achievements. You will see how you are happily "on your way" to increasing your achievements.

You must believe our offer will actually work for you, with NO RISK! We guarantee "no risk" because, in humans, FEAR OF LOSS IS STRONGER THAN DESIRE FOR GAIN, so we must take away any risk that could be involved; we will even give you the subjects to talk about. It's all done for you; how about that?

AND WE GUARANTEE IT! WHAT COULD BE BETTER THAN THAT?

We must show you the many ways to get UNDERLINE DRESSED UP AND

................................OUT! On your FIST DATE – WITHIN 7 DAYS.

"MAGIC GRAND SLAM OFFER"

With this offer, a premium price, and an unbeatable guarantee, we are able to make a Winner out of you! We are presenting our offer, one which cannot be compared to any other products or services available, by promoting an unmatchable guarantee; this allows you to feel confident in the propositions presented in this, yours and our, book.

"GRAND SLAM OFFER" – "GSO"

The "GSO" increases the belief in your book, increases your response, makes your book and its ideas seem new, different, "Value"-driven versus "Price"- driven.

WOW! We just found our new business – Showing Lonely Women and Men how "Not to be Lonely any longer!!" Our "STARVING CROWD" is the reader of our book. People who have pain and want and need a companion. Our starving crowd is Growing!

Did you know that there are more people turning 65 every year than there are turning 20 this year? Talk about a "Starving Audience". Growing! Growing! Growing!

When you see or hear that we have the "Solution to your pain of Loneliness," you will be living proof that this book works!

You, our Reader, are definitely understood.

LET'S BEGIN!

You have associates who belong to:

Clubs

Groups

Mailing lists

Social Media Groups

Use them to get the word around. You are sincerely and urgently looking for a:

Soulmate

Friend

Companion

Man!

The faster and more clearly you can demonstrate this benefit are accruing, the more valuable.

Now is the time to start looking at least 2 – 3 Dating Sites. We have listed them and given our opinion, so pick out at least two (some are "free!"), join them, pick, and "get in touch." Your phone will start ringing, listen, I heat it!

When you tell anyone, ANYONE, your story, hand out at least 3 – 4 Business Cards for them to distribute to their acquaintances.

FAST BEATS FREE!

In a market competing against FREE – YOU NEED TO DOUBLE DOWN ON SPEED!

Increase the value (Dream) while decreasing (Time Delay) and the (Effort and Sacrifice.)

<u>Dream of Outcome Belief of Likelihood of Achievement</u>

Time Delay, Effort, and Sacrifice

Do this, and YOU will Win The Game.

Values versus what is good for ME!

ME is the KEY!

These "goals" have all been addressed, and now you will have a lot of ideas and subjects to talk about.

We found out our customers' desires, then devised how many ways we could create value – NOW LET'S DO IT! GO ALL IN!!

GO ALL IN!!

When you're thinking about your "Dream" outcome, it has to be YOU arriving at YOUR destination and what it would be like to experience that.

Have a Growing market with a Grand Slam Offer.

"STARVING CROWS"

Our target is women who have pain and want a fun companion. Our Market is Growing!

When you learn or hear the solution to the pain, you will feel understood. You must have a painful problem for us to solve, and we have solved it for you in this book. Check out the Volunteer, Meeting and Dating Sites coming up – enjoy!

The faster and more clearly you can demonstrate this benefit you are accruing, the more valuable.

TIP – FAST BEATS FREE!!

You are paying the price for value, SPEED

Your value versus what is good for ME. ME is the KEY!

We have found out your desires, and then devised how many ways we could create value for you – now.

Go All In!

Go to the Internet or local printer, Staples, Office Depot. Order 500 sexy Business Cards that have only your name and phone number (a snappy saying if you have one). Don't forget your picture if you have a good one. Idea! Years ago, I had a picture of me sitting in front of the fireplace on the rug, petting my dog. Cozy, huh? Just an idea.

No address. If you have a professional picture, you really like, then be sure to use it (with your new make-up and hairstyle). (Remember: No address, No Company Name, Stay Safe!) Have fun getting your business cars; you are in "the business" of "getting your man!"

We have found out our customers' desires and then devised how many ways we could create value.

What is your goal now? To keep your appointments in Week #1 is your Goal! Your goal now is to be perceived as Beautiful and Successful.

After several of our friends and successful people tell you how great you look, believe them and start showing it in your carriage!

So, FIRST – KEEP ALL YOUR APPOINTMENTS

Did you know that some cities have schools and colleges that teach all the beauty needs and to do them at a much lower cost? Give them a try!

Hairstylist:

Go to the Internet magazines, study new styles, decide on one or two, and talk to your stylist about them for you. Make an appointment with your stylist and try out your favorite. Have fun – this is supposed to be fun!

Nails, Fingers, and Toes:

Have your fingernails a little bit longer than usual with bright red nail polish and one fingernail GOLD!

Make-up (by a professional):

Don't forget your new eyelashes! Make an appointment and GO!

When you find your make-up, hair, and nail stylists, give us a call, and we will negotiate with the businesses where you are going to get your hair and nails done and negotiate with them. We have a very good negotiating team – give us a try.

START throwing away your old clothes and/or sharing them with your relatives and friends. They will get excited and increase your level of excitement when they realize what YOU are doing – "getting you man!"

Throw away or share clothes that are:

    Old

    Outdated

    Torn

    Ripped

Holey

Do not fit!

Faded.

Shoes that are Old

Scuffed

Beyond looking at!

Buy new shoes:

Highest Heel you can comfortably.

Buy sandals that have a small heel, white or silver!

Buy new clothes or fix your older ones. But sure they are

WHITE (Magic color!)

Or – Mainly white with

Bright colors featured:

Pink

Yellow

Blue

Frilly

Lacy

Sparkly

Shiny!

Lingerie:

Lacy

White

Pink

TRY BLACK!! WOW!

Talk to 3-5 people every day, even if you have to go to a store to do it. Talk towomen, men, children, anyone they have:

Husband

Brothers

Uncles

Friend.

Get a cute, sweet dog; if you don't have time (or a place) for a dog, offer to walk a neighbor's dog for 4 weeks. Strike up a conversation with everyone who is "walking their dog," compliment their dog, and pat him (if he's little)

Tell everyone about your "mission" and what you are doing to ensure it happens. All this is necessary because you want to be perceived as beautiful, pretty, shapely, and sexy. To be perceived as powerful in what you do!

Give everyone you talk to 3 – 5 Business Cards and ask to hand them out to their friends. Pick out a pretty pattern. People will be interested in your story, tell it, make it interesting, and embellish it up a bit! Make it, so other people want to repeat it! Your phone will be <u>"Ringing Off the Hook!"</u>

Everyone has associates who belong to:

> Clubs
>
> Groups
>
> Mailing lists
>
> Social media groups
>
> Next, keep appointments for:
>
> Hairstyle
>
> Nail done, Hands and toes
>
> Make-up (don't forget – try on some false eyelashes and
>
>> see how you like them, pretty, huh?)

clothes:

> One-shoulder
>
> Off-the-shoulder
>
> Straps
>
> Lots if WHITE
>
> Pink
>
> Yellow

Bright colors, mixed onto a White background

Shorten your hems, don't forget; men like to see skin, shoulders, and especially, legs.

All this is necessary because you want to be perceived as beautiful, shapely, sexy, etc., to be perceived as powerful in what you do.

<u>WEEK #1, VOLUNTEER, MEETINGS, and DATING SITES.</u>

<u>(Don't forget political meetings, if those are your interests. They are always busy with projects.)</u>

Go to Volunteer, Committee Meetings.

JOIN Dating Sites (listed at the end of this page.)

Check out the ones you are interested in – then CALL, VOLUNTEER, AND/OR JOIN!

Pick and Commit!

Call them on the telephone or research them on the Internet. Volunteers, Phone Numbers, Websites (Check out the local Chamber of Commerce, get lists with Phone Numbers_____

_____

Where they meet – Time:

_____

Professional Meetings

_____
_____

Where they meet – Time:

_____

When did they meet?

_____

Find one or two you like. Try to find several that meet this week. When you go to the Committee Meetings, talk to everyone you meet and tell them what you are seeking, give everyone you talk to 3-5 Business Cards and ask them to hand them out to their relatives and friends:

Fathers

Brothers

Uncles

Cousins

Friends

Who are ALL LONELY?

GIVE IT A TRY!

Call and JOIN. Attend the first meeting you find that fits your schedule.

Same way with the Meeting Committee. Follow the same guidelines, pick, and commit!

Next, check out these DATING SITES for the ones that interest you. Pick 2 or 3 and join (some are free – check)! These are very important. Pick and commit!

Don't forget Judy and Colin at the beginning of the book – they met on a Dating Site and recognized immediately that they were soulmates! It could happen to you!

It happened to Tom and me, also, so here are two examples. Bet there are hundreds, thousands out there, bet? Call us when it happens, and we will put you in our next book, don't forget!)

DRESS UP (HEELS) ....AND...................GO!!

DATING SITES – on the Internet:

   1. *Over 50 Crowd:*

"OurTime.com" for older singles looking to connect for love and companionship.

   2. *"eHarmony.com"*

3. *"SilverSingles.com"*:

Over 50s is the fastest-growing group of subscribers for online dating.

4. *"Meetup.com"*:

Find groups with shared interests.

5. *"Senior Centers"*:

Offer to volunteer. Donate your time to area thrift stores that donate only to hospice. There are thousands of opportunities to meet and help others. Senior Center offers educational classes, day trips, and other social opportunities and trips.

DRESS UP......AND.......Go – Don't forget those wedges – easy to walk in also!

6. *Check out "workforce50.com"*:

Features specifically for older workers as well as resources for a mid-life change.

7. *"Seniorjobbank.org"*:

8. *"AARP.org/work."*

A great wat to meet fellow seniors.

9. *"Seniorjournal.com"*:

Be social for your health.

Experts say, "Seniors with a high level of activity are twice as likely to remain free of a disability."

10. Move to a <u>Retirement Community:</u>

Improve your dating pool! Lots of potential mates reside. Stress-free lifestyle, enjoy private tennis courts, and swimming pools, and look for Mr. Right sipping wine at Clubhouse!

11. Check out <u>"Retirementliving.com"</u>:

for retirement communities in your area.

12. <u>"DatingAdvice.com"</u>:

Has completed a list of Top 6 ways to meet seniors. Browse the list, plus some that we have added:

A. *<u>"eHarmony.com"</u> –* casual dates, deep relationships, Number 1 trusted Dating App. Every 14 minutes, one falls in love on eHarmony.com This could be you!!

B. *<u>"EliteSingles.com"</u> –* caters to highly educated uses an advanced system to make sure everyone is who he says he is.

C. *<u>"Match.com"</u> -* has more "Over 50" members than any other dating service. Has a simple matching process.

D. *<u>"Ourtime.com"</u> –* has the most people.

E. *<u>"SilverSingles.com"</u> –* has lots of class!

F. Over 70 – *<u>"EliteSingles"</u>* – designed for the Cream of the Crop of the Dating World.

G. *<u>"ChristianMingle"</u> –* Catholic Seniors.

H. *<u>"Jdate"</u> –* Jewish Singles

Important Tips:

Safety first

Meet in well-lit public places.

Don't limit your options.

Take your time.

When answering an advertisement, pay your selection a compliment. Be specific in your message:

Start by pointing out things you like about the person's profile or things that you have in common.

Always by pointing out things you like about the person's profile or things that you have in common.

Be sure and get the cost down before joining. Good luck!! Have fun!! Let us hear from you. (1-321-536-6555).

Now that's Done, time to do:

WEEK #1 – GET "DOWN AND DIRTY" and MAKE YOURSELF BEAUTIFUL!!

Don't forget everybody likes pretty, clean, neat, well-dressed women. And your Increased Status within your group of friends will increase your confidence in yourself. These are powerful drives use them to make your mission SUCCESSFUL!

MAGIC "GRAND SLAM OFFER" ("GSO")

Tom and I will assist you with help writing your bio for the dating site, if needed, or anything within our power to "Get Your Man."

A Grand Slam Offer is an offer that cannot be compared to any other product or service available. Our Grand Slam Offer promotes an unmatchable guarantee.

A Grand Slam Offer increases your response. Most people will be attracted when they see a "Grand Slam Offer." A "Grand Slam Offer" makes this book seem new, different, and VALUE-driven versus PRICE-driven.

You are a member of our "STARVING CROWD."

People who have pain, the power to do things, and are easy to target; this group is growing every day - this is good news for you the: "GSO" Woman on a Mission!

The "GSO woman" must feel understood, confident that her "mission" will be successful, confident that her social status has increased enough to make her attractive inside and outside. The faster and more clearly we can demonstrate these benefits that are accruing, the more valuable!

Reduce the bottom line, and your Effort and Sacrifice is "0". YOU WIN THE GAME!!

TIP - FAST BEATS FREE! There is value in Value and Speed. In a market competing against FREE, YOU MUST DOUBLE DOWN ON SPEED!

People value SUCCESS versus "What is good for ME. ME is the KEY!

<u>Type</u>

Once-in-a-while man

Partner

Live-in

Live out

Stay overnight

Stay overnight once in a while

Never stay Overnight

 Stay overnight once in a while
Never Goes Home (He's probably "not in the running, right?)

Neat

Good Conversationalist

Decent Looking

No bad habits

Drinking, excessively

Drinking, moderately

No swearing

Burping (or the other direction)

Thinks of MY comforts all the time

Thinks of MY comfort most of the time

Thinks of My comforts never (You don't want to be bothered with him!)

He:

Has a car

Clean

Decent Running

Decent Looking

Good Driver

Safety Conscious

Non-speeder

Courteous Driver

Opens car door

Polite

Courteous

Nice to your friends

Two more things –

NEVER TALK ABOUT your small kids, unless he has small kids to talk about himself, and (this is important) HE brings it up!

Never talks about his Ex-wife! Be it good or bad!

What do "YOU" REALLY WANT?

Soulmate

Friend

Companion

Man!!

Destination: To be attractive to the men who interest you.

MAKE APPOINTMENTS – ALL IN THE FIRST WEEK AND GO GET BEAUTIFUL:

Hair Stylist.

Go to the internet magazines, study new styles, decide on two or three, and talk to your stylist about them. Make an appointment with your stylist and try out your favorite!

Make an appointment: Nails, Fingers, and Toes.

Have fingernails a little bit longer than usual with bright red polish and one fingernail GOLD! Professional Make-up Artist, Make appointment..........and..........GO!

Go shopping for dresses.

> Look on the computer and see some of the latest styles. Pick and Commit: White, white background with pretty flowers, or colors in it, swishy, flowery, long, short, or medium. If too long, get out your needle and thread and hem them up! Then hem them up again, don't forget men like to seeskin – let's them know they are alive!!!

Shoes

> Buy as high heels as you are comfortable wearing. If you don't wear heels, search for a "wedgie" platform shoe that will make your legs look longer, sleeker, and sexier! Buy pretty white or silver sandals. Then, get your toes painted the same color as your nails.

Lingerie

> Pretty

> Dainty

> Lacy

> Pink

> White

> Flowers

> WOW – BLACK!

> Lacy thing (if you like the style), pretty

> Underthings, don't forget sexy bras!

Meanwhile: <u>THROW AWAY:</u>

>Old comfy clothes

>Faded

>Stained

>Holes (especially blue jeans)

>Don't fit!

BUY or sew yourself (or hire a seamstress)

>NEW CLOTHES:

>Dresses

>Light, color, and fabric (Don't forget WHITE, MAGIC!)

>Bright

>Swishy

>Fluffy, ruffled

>One-shoulder

>Off-the-shoulder

>Straps

>Lots of White

Pink

Yellow

Bright colors mixed onto a White background with a shorter hem.

Shoes

The highest hell you can wear (at least one high-heel pair),

Sandals, mostly white or silver

Jewelry

That matches clothes: necklaces and Dangly earrings.

VOLUNTEER:

Research, search all the Volunteer Venues you can find, pick out two.

Select the ones that you feel will attract mostly men (That's who we are "hunting" - RIGHT?

Give them a RING and VOLUNTEER!

Pick out 2 dating sites and go out on 2 dates at least a week (if possible).

Go to at least two Volunteer Venues a week, preferably on different days and times of the day (or night)!

DRESS UP (Wear Heels) Pick and Commit.......... And................GO!

MEETINGS:

Research all the Meetings that are a mixed (men and women) Groups, preferably an AFTER-SUPPER MEETING.

Political meetings sometimes have Galas in the evening where men will be looking for a date.

Look over the DATING SITES, pick a couple, and check out how much they cost(some are free).

Value versus what is good for you

Women value a good:

Man

Friend

Companion!

This is what they need; this is what this book provides in order to give them what they really need.

When you go to a volunteer meeting, committee meeting, or to a dating site, be sure to talk to a lot of people, tell them your story, and your Mission - looking for a man!

Talk to at least 3-5 men every day!! EVERY DAY!!

Postman

Milkman

Neighbor

Stranger on the sidewalk

Walking their dog!

Decide to accept every date when you are asked.

Get a "fancy" calendar to keep in your pocket. Take it out and peruse the dates, looking for the date when your gentleman friend asked you for his date.

Double check! Then write the time, place, man's phone number, type of date, movie, dinner, etc.

IN SPARE TIME

At night, during lunch, or at suppertime, look at, cut out, write down styles you like, order, go to stores, try on for size, style looks, likes, dresses, outfits, Knock 'em Dead Clothes!

REMEMBER

Meet your date at a public place, Restaurant, Movie, Library, etc. Never go in a car with a stranger until you have met him in a public place and decided he was valuable.

DRESS UP (with high heels) ....and........................GO!

"Lonely women"

Women who want a:

Soulmate

Friend

Companion

Man!

WIN-WIN!!

MAGIC "GRAND SLAM" OFFER INCREASES VALUE:

A Category of one with no comparison.

OFFER: Present to the Marketplace an offer that cannot be compared to any other product or service available, combining an attractive promotion, an unmatchable value.

Get a Deal -The reason people try anything IS to get a Deal!!

You will have a woman who feels understood, confident that her mission will be successful, and confident that her social status will increase enough to make her attractive inside and outside! Pick a specific type of man that reverses your deepest fears! Pick, then Commit!

YOUR NEW MOTTO IS:

"DRESS UP (WEAR HIGH HEELS) ....and.. ....GO!"

Reduce the "Time Delay," and your "Effort and Sacrifice" (DRESS UP AND....GO) is "WIN"! Well worth the time and expense, RIGHT?

YOU WIN THE GAME!!

"GSO" only becomes valuable once you perceive the increase in "likelihood of achievement, perceive the decrease in Time Delay in effort and Sacrifice. Think about psychological solutions rather than logical ones!

Accurately depicting that DREAM back for you, so you feel understood, and we explain how our book will get you there.

STATUS is important; this book will get you there before you realize it. Friends will be asking, "Where did you meet HIM? How did you find HIM?

Women want to be perceived as:

Beautiful

Respected

Powerful

Loved

Increased Status

These are powerful drives, and you have them!

<u>GO! - USE THOSE DRIVES!</u>

<u>DRESS UP..........and..........................GO!</u>

To church. Stay afterward and have a cup of coffee. Talk to everyone, male and female. And, if you know some of the ladies, tell them your story about the "fun mission" you are on how much time you have to "get it done." Just 30 days! (less a few already, don't forget!)

Ask if they know any men around your age who are lonely, and might like company:

Widowed father

Uncle

Brother

Neighbor

And don't forget, hand out at least 3 Business Cards to everyone you speak to.

Think hard for anyone someone might know. Ask everyone you speak to.

Make appointments to attend a Dance Class evening or late afternoon (near suppertime). Early evening is great because they will sometimes ask you to have supper right from Dance Class!

Go to mid-week and weekend Dance Classes and/or parties.

DRESS UP (WEAR HEELS).........................AND..........GO!

Be a Conversationalist! Go to the Library, look at men's magazines, or better yet, go to a bookstore (you might see a man there). Look at the pictures - hunting, fishing, sports, anything, and everything - you will be armed with every conversion you could enter.

Dance with everyone who asks you, at least once!

Pick 3 or 4 subjects and read about: gardening, motorcycling, cooking, dancing, swimming, running, sailing, boating, fishing, Football, etc. Bone up on 2 or 3 of these ideas, and your conversation will keep you going all evening!

Check out Singles Groups and JOIN!

Men's interests: Family, History, Long Ago History, Cars, Boats, Golfing, Tennis sports, fishing, etc.

Look in magazines, newspapers, and local pamphlets, write a witty ad "looking for a date" and place the ad in the place you have decided upon, put your phone number in big letters. Wait, your phone will be ringing-watch!

Practice smiling in the mirror. Make sure when your lips smile, that your eyes smile also. Make up your eyes! Make them sparkle while you drink wine, converse, and talk.

JOIN: Playing Card Groups. Bridge, Pinochle, Eucre, Poker.

JOIN Bowling Leagues, these types of sports really interest men. If you don't bowl, at least go to the Bowling Alley and watch, holler, at least - join in!!

When you meet your man, be sure:

He is neat

Powerful

Safe driver

Temperate Drinker

For many men, making "Money" is more important than being "handsome" (and that type may appeal to you also. Keep your eyes open!)

Their Status, professionally and socially. Study this man; what about him do you especially like? Is he nice? You're nice - maybe you are a match?

Weeks #2, #3, and #4 - Repeat ALL the meetings and Dating Sites and handout cards - you will meet more men than you ever imagined.

Doing all the options we have suggested, you might think –

PROBLEMS

These things are too HARD CONFUSING (I might not like it)

Takes too much TIME

Takes too much MONEY

Too HARD

Not WORTH it

Won't WORK

Won't be able to STICK with it

Will SUCK at it

I am BUSY

Won't be CONVENIENT for me

The more problems you have, the more you get to solve! Fun! Fun!

Take each problem, and reverse each element of the obstacle to solutionoriented language! ADD: "HOW TO SOLVE!" Get your friends involved in "the hunt!" Remember, when you are done "finding your man," it will have been worth every minute, every PENNY!

When you go to a Volunteer and/or Committee Meeting, tell everyone who you talk to that you are looking for:

A Man

Soulmate

Friend

Companion!

Tell your story every day to the:

Postman

Milkman

Neighbor

A stranger on the sidewalk,

A stranger walking their dog!

Decide to accept every date when you are asked.

Put the date, time, and place in your fancy calendar to keep in your pocket. Take it out and peruse the dates, looking for the day when your gentleman friend has asked you for his date. Write the man's name and Phone #, type of date: movie, dinner, walk, etc.)

Remember: Never meet anywhere except in a Public Place, Restaurant, Movie, Library, etc.

Never go in a car until you have met him in a public place and decided he is possibly valuable.

DRESS UP (IN HIGH HEELS) and GO!

"Lonely Woman who wants to meet a man! WIN – WIN

Don't forget - there are as many men OUT THERE as there are women who are "Lonely," who would like to have a:

Friend

Companion

An interesting Woman like YOU!

The Perfect Audience!!

You have been the PERFECT AUDIENCE. You have gotten Beautiful; you have gotten "Out in the World!" You have let everyone know about your "fun mission"! I imagine your telephone is Ringing "Off The Hook" right now!

If not, Do the Volunteer, Meeting Exercises, and Dating Siters (pick a couple of new ones again and go meet:

Men

Friends

Companions

Soul Mates

Your man is "out there!" GO - find him! You know how – just DO IT!

Good Luck and remember WHAT YOU DID when you GET your New Man, Remember HOW YOU DID IT, so repeat it every day to KEEP your new man, and you will have your "SOUL MATE! Enjoy.

Sincerely, Tom and Joan McCormack (Married Soul-Mates for 26 years) and still very happy and interested!! It worked for us and will work for you - GUARANTEED!!

ENJOY YOUR NEW LIFE, FULL OF EXCITEMENT AND LOVE!

To Our Dear Reader,

Tell every person when you find your man- let us know – tell us your story. (321-536-6555).

We will put your picture and story in our next book.

Tom and I look forward to hearing from you soon!!

Sincerely,

With Love!!!

BEST WISHES TO YOU

www.ingramcontent.com/pod-product-compliance
Lightning Source LLC
Chambersburg PA
CBHW051247120626
46547CB00014B/1834

*9 7 8 1 9 6 4 9 2 9 5 1 4 *